# A vision for mission

## FOSTER R. McCURLEY

Library of Congress Catalog Card Number: 87-083062

Printed in the United States of America

ISBN: 0-936536-06-3


Cover Design: Michael W. Young Associates, Inc.

# Contents

# Foreword

"A Vision for Mission" is a study paper commissioned by the Division for Mission in North America of the Lutheran Church in America. The author, Foster R. McCurley, has served with the staff of the division as a teacher and counselor in the area of biblical research and study on mission, and as chairperson of the Church in Society unit.

The purpose of this paper is to provide biblical/theological definition, intent, and understanding of the positions and experience of the Lutheran Church in America, particularly in mission in North America. Beyond this initial purpose, the division believes that the paper can serve as a valuable transition document as the DMNA/LCA provides for the transfer of its responsibilities to at least six of the churchwide units in the Evangelical Lutheran Church in America.

The division's approach to mission has been to view our task comprehensively as we in the community of faith

—witness to the Gospel;
—proclaim the message of and in Christ's name;
—provide for the care of others through the maintenance of a social service system;

—advocate on behalf of members of the human family so that they may experience human fulfillment and justice;

—acknowledge, welcome, encourage, and interact with work done by others, both publicly and privately, for the good of the human community.

Without presumption we say that we in the church participate in the mission that is God's. God calls us, redeems us, and leads us by the Spirit in ministry among and with all people in the world—the objects of divine love.

Mission is perceived by the church within the context of its experience of the kingdom that has come and its vision of the kingdom yet to come. It is here that we live and carry out our ministry as committed disciples with the hope-filled vision of God for all people. Our ministry is always that of the "servant people," and the cross is our paradigm.

"A Vision for Mission" defines this church's mission in North America. It relates particularly to the areas of the church's ministry for which the Division for Mission in North America has been responsible. In fact, the paper serves as the centerpiece around which a description of, and strategies for, the ministries and activities of the DMNA can be interpreted.

It is the intention of the DMNA that the use of this study paper will be of value

—to many in the church, helping them to understand the meaning of mission, particularly our mission in North America, as perceived by the LCA at this time;

—to the successor churchwide units of DMNA as a document around which strategies for ministry may be developed which are consistent in their policy and understanding of mission;

—to the synods of the LCA as they engage in the interpretation of strategies for mission—comprehensive and inclusive—on their territories, and as they provide materials for transition to the newly organized synods of the ELCA;

—to those areas—in city, town, and country—where pastors, congregations, and directors of ministry engage in the use of the "principles for parish ministry" in each place; and

—to all who seek, however humbly, to participate in the mission that is God's.

Thanks be to God for the call to participate in God's mission in the world.

Executive Director                 KENNETH C. SENFT
Division for Mission in North America
Lutheran Church in America

# Introduction

## THE MISSION OF GOD AND
## THE NATURE OF THE CHURCH

While Christians employ the word "mission" in a variety of ways to speak of what the church is to do on God's behalf in the world, it is striking that the word "mission" does not appear anywhere in the Bible, the Lutheran Confessions, or the ancient creeds of the church. Without clear documentation for the use of the word, there seems to be little consensus about its precise meaning in terms of whose mission it is, how broadly or narrowly this mission is to be understood, and what forms the mission should take.

The English word "mission" is a noun which is used in a variety of ways. A group of persons in the act of representing their government is on a "mission." Likewise, a task given to an individual or group (specifically, a military task assigned by higher headquarters) is a "mission." A body of persons sent by a church to carry on religious work is also on a "mission," and the word further designates the place where such persons function. In addition, a place for humanitarian or philanthropic work can be called a "mission." In general English usage, then, the word refers to people, a task, or a place.

"Mission" is derived from a Latin verb meaning "to send." The Old and New Testaments abound in various forms of verbs meaning "to send." This is typical of biblical expression (particularly on the basis of the Hebrew language), where greater emphasis is placed on verbs than on nouns. Particularly significant for a theological study of mission are the hundreds of cases where God or Christ is the subject of the verb "send." God *sent* Joseph to preserve life in Egypt, Moses and Aaron to deliver the people from bondage there, Nathan to reprove David for killing Uriah, an angel to save Jerusalem under siege, prophets to proclaim the word of God in terms of judgment and of salvation and comfort, the word itself to bring blessings on Jerusalem. God *sent* John to bear witness to the light, messengers to preach, an angel to rescue Peter from prison. God *sent* Jesus Christ, the only Son of God, to justify ungodly humanity, to provide life through him, to be the expiation for our sins, to be the Savior of the world. God *sent* the Holy Spirit, through whom the good news might be preached.

As God sent Jesus into the world, so Jesus Christ *sent* his apostles to preach the nearness of the kingdom of God, to heal the sick, raise the dead, cleanse lepers, cast out demons, and enable the world to know God and Christ. Christ *sent* Paul to preach the gospel to the Gentiles. Indeed, the word "apostle" means nothing other than "one who is sent."

This survey of the biblical usage of "sending" makes abundantly clear that God is the "Sender" of various persons in order to preserve life, to reprove, to deliver, to save, to proclaim the word as judgment and salvation, to bear witness, to justify, to inspire. Having been sent, Christ is the "Sender" of apostles to announce the kingdom of God in word and deed, to preach the gospel where it is not known.

Theologically, then, "mission" (literally, "sending") is the work of God by which God reaches out to the world in order to effect the divine will. Therefore, one can speak of "the mission of the church" only in the most literal meaning of the word "apostolic": sent. Perhaps, in order to avoid the impression that the church is the sender, the initiator, the designer, or the sole proprietor, one should speak rather of "the mission of God" in which the church participates by being sent into God's world.

What is the nature of the church, and what is its role in God's mission?

The seventh article of the Unaltered Augsburg Confession offers a definition of the church which has been considered by many to represent the most ecumenical definition possible:

> It is also taught among us that one holy Christian church will be and remain forever. This is the assembly of all believers among whom the Gospel is preached in its purity and the holy sacraments are administered according to the Gospel. (Theodore G. Tappert, ed. and trans., **The Book of Concord: The Confessions of the Evangelical Lutheran Church** [Philadelphia: Fortress Press, 1959], p. 39.1-2. **Note:** All following references to the Lutheran Confessions are from this work.)

This definition expresses what constitutes the church, what distinguishes its membership from other groups, and what criterion is used to make that distinction. Furthermore, this understanding of the church is truly ecumenical, for it excludes no gathering, no organized assembly, no denomination, except by the criterion of the purity of the gospel in terms of preaching and as the basis for administering the sacraments.

This understanding of the church continues the tradition of the ecumenical creeds. The Apostles' Creed identifies the church simply and concisely as "the holy catholic church, the communion of saints." The terms "holy" and "catholic" accomplish simultaneously the "separateness" of the church and its "universal" character. The church is not identical to the world, but distinct in the world; yet the church is worldwide, inclusive of all peoples, languages, colors, and races. Furthermore, the apposition "the communion of saints" indicates that the church consists of those who have been justified by the cross of Jesus Christ and who therefore confess Jesus Christ as Lord.

In his Small Catechism, Luther explains the third article of this creed by comparing the individual's confession to the experience of the whole church:

> I believe that by my own reason or strength I cannot believe in Jesus Christ, my Lord, or come to him. But the Holy Spirit has called me through the Gospel, enlightened me with his gifts, and sanctified and preserved me in the true faith, just as he calls, gathers, enlightens, and sanctifies the whole Christian church on earth and preserves it in union with Jesus Christ in the one true faith (Tappert, p. 345.6).

Furthermore, in his Large Catechism Luther discusses more specifically the phrase "communion of saints":

> This is the sum and substance of this phrase: I believe that there is on earth a little holy flock or community of pure saints under one head, Christ. It is called together by the Holy Spirit in one faith, mind, and understanding. It possesses a variety of gifts, yet is united in love without sect or schism. Of this community I also am a part and member, a participant and co-partner in all the blessings it possesses (Tappert, p. 417.51ff.).

In this way Luther develops the notion of the sharing of life, of goods, and of the troubles of members with one another.

The Nicene Creed defines the church as "one, holy, catholic, and apostolic." Added to the formula of the Apostles' Creed are the words "one" (which attests to the church's unity on the basis of faith) and "apostolic" (which bases that faith on the preaching of those who were eyewitnesses to the resurrection of Jesus Christ).

Thus the content of faith proclaimed through the tradition of the church becomes the criterion which distinguishes the church from other gatherings, even from other religious groups.

Given these definitions of the church, it is clear that a discussion of the church's participation in God's mission must begin with the task of preaching and teaching that faith—given by God through the Holy Spirit—in every time and place. If the church is defined by its God-given, Spirit-inspired, and verbally proclaimed faith, then the essential task of the church is obviously to preach and teach that which constitutes itself: the gospel. Without the gospel—promised in the Old Testament and proclaimed through the apostolic witness of the New Testament—the church does not and cannot exist.

Such an understanding of the essential role to which God calls the church is consistent with the biblical witness. One of the biblical passages most frequently quoted in defining the church is that powerful formula addressed to the Christians in Asia Minor:

> But you are a chosen race, a royal priesthood, a holy nation, God's own people, that you may declare the wonderful deeds of him who brought you out of darkness into his marvelous light. Once you were no people, but now you are God's people. Once you had not received mercy, but now you have received mercy.
>
> (1 Peter 2:9-10)

The declarative terms are derived from a passage which originally defined Israel, God's people in the Old Testament (Exodus 19:5-6). Israel's identity was based upon the prior saving act of God in the exodus from Egypt. Her role as "a holy nation" and "a kingdom of priests" was the consequence of what God "did to the Egyptians." As a result of God's salvation, Israel was not isolated from the world, but instead called to God's mission in the world, "for all the earth is mine." In other words, because God the Creator reigns over the entire earth, Israel, the redeemed community, has a particular role to play: to obey God's voice and keep the covenant established at Mount Sinai. In this way Israel would demonstrate her holiness, that is, her distinctiveness in the world, and would play the priestly roles of mediator and teacher.

When applied to the Christian community in Asia Minor, those same declarative terms share a similar basis: God's salvation. What is strikingly different, however, is that salvation is now accomplished in the cross of Christ, and also that the Christian response is described in terms of witnessing: "[in order] that you may declare." It is the church's witness to the gospel that replaces Israel's commitment to keep the covenant. It is that gospel's proclamation which is necessary for faith (Romans 10:17), and it is through that proclamation of Christ crucified and resurrected that God calls into being a new people. Thus the church's responsibility to proclaim the gospel —the constitutive and definitive role of the church in the ecumenical creeds and in the Lutheran Confessions—has its basis in Holy Scripture.

The birth of the church on the day of Pentecost raises another aspect of the church's nature which is crucial for understanding its role in God's mission. On that day the strange phenomenon occurred in which, following the gift of the Holy Spirit, the Galilean apostles of Jesus Christ were heard to speak in other languages. To meet the assumption that the apostles were intoxicated, Peter quoted scriptural prophecy:

> And in the last days it shall be, God declares, that I will pour out my Spirit upon all flesh, and your sons and your daughters shall prophesy.

> (Joel 2:28ff.)

The apostle's explanation indicates that "the last days" had arrived, that the expected reign of God had dawned. The proof of such fulfillment was the gift of the Spirit by which prophecy was reawakened.

In order to comprehend the significance of the fulfillment of that prophecy for God's mission and the nature of the church, we must allow Holy Scripture to interpret itself. These writings, which are normative for our understanding of the word of God, present us with a comprehensive witness to God as Creator, Redeemer, and Sanctifier, and to the role of God's people in creation, redemption, and sanctification.

# CHAPTER 1

# The Reign of God Over Creation

The Bible's opening chapters establish the crucial theological premises about creation—the arena in which God's mission takes place. Genesis 1, written in its final form in the sixth century B.C., and Genesis 2, completed in final form in the tenth century B.C., were both statements to their own day about the world as God created it to be. Each story is a profound witness to the Creator God in terms of the situations in which the people of Israel lived. The writers of these chapters described God's creative work on the basis of long-standing traditions and the best scientific knowledge of the day. Yet what we possess from their pens is not so much a scientific explanation about the origin of things as it is a faith response to the role of God as Ruler over the world.

## The Order of God's Creation

A theological understanding of the creation stories in the Bible might best be stated in terms of the relationships which God established in the beginning. When the content of these relationships continues, the result for God's world will be creation wholeness and harmony—what the Israelites called *shalom*. In Genesis 1 and 2, there are basically four such relationships, each with its own content:

1) **The relationship of God to the world** is basic to all others, for it is defined by the initial act of God: overcoming chaos ("formlessness and waste" [Genesis 1:2] in the forms of darkness, water, and wind) with the order of light, land, vegetation, heavenly luminaries, fish, fowl, land beasts, and, eventually, humans. The content of this relationship is based upon the proper functioning of each created phenomenon in the order of things. The function of the light is to separate night and day, that of the land to produce cultivatable crops, that of the crops to reproduce themselves; the luminaries serve to give light and to separate days, seasons, and years. God's reign is established upon this principle of order, and insofar as each phenomenon serves its purpose and thus contributes to the whole, God declares it to be good. This evaluation of created matter as "good" (Hebrew *tob*), indeed of the whole of creation as "very good," is essential to the entire biblical story, and distinguishes the biblical faith from several other major religions of the world.

2) **The relationship of God to humans** is likewise unusual in comparison with other religious expressions. The two stories at the beginning of Genesis portray God as working at great length to prepare a decent neighborhood for humans. The author of Genesis 1 describes the creation of the vast, orderly universe as the arena in which God creates humanity, while the storyteller of Genesis 2 indicates a much more local scene, a virtual oasis, which God establishes as a habitat for the human. In these two stories the provisions made by God include not only the necessities of life such as land, water, light, and food, but also things which delight the eyes and, above all, the gift of sociality: "It is not good that the man should be alone." There can be no *shalom* without companionship and sociality.

Yet the most powerful and profound statement regarding the relationship of God and humans lies in Genesis 1: "Let us make man in our image, after our likeness" (1:26). That human beings present to the world the "image of God" bestows on the likes of every one of us a dignity which surpasses all understanding:

> When I look at the heavens, the work of thy fingers,
>> the moon and the stars which thou hast established;
>> what is man that thou art mindful of him,
>> and the son of man that thou dost care for him?
> Yet thou hast made him little less than God,
>> and dost crown him with glory and honor.

> (Psalm 8:3-5)

Since the creation of humans in God's image occurs before and apart from the biblical development of races, languages, and nations, it is clear that there can be no claim to inherent superiority by one group over others. People of all nations, races, and religions have the same worth in the eyes of God.

Strikingly, the identity or importance of humankind is not, as is true of the rest of creation, based upon function. Rather, it is the relationship of humans to God "in God's image" which establishes one's identity as a human being. The function or responsibility which humans play follows, rather than forms, the basis for this identity.

3) **The relationship of humans to the world** is simultaneously one of work and responsibility, particularly when the creation accounts of Genesis 1 and 2 are taken together. The author of Genesis 1 assigns humanity "dominion" over the rest of the creatures. While that assignment has often been interpreted solely in light of the negative sounding "subdue" which follows, clearly "dominion" has to do with the role of royalty in caring for a kingdom. It is a matter of nurture and guidance rather than oppression; it is an assignment of royal responsibility rather than aristocratic privilege. In any case, human dominion over creation has as its purpose the maintenance of orderliness in the world. It is nothing less than the stewardship of God's creatures for the purpose of attaining *shalom* for all.

3

In a more local way, the author of Genesis 2 discusses the relationship of humans to the world in terms of the occupations known in the Palestinian countryside. After God had worked to create the garden, the man was given the task of tilling and keeping the soil in order to experience the fruits of his labors (Genesis 2:15). This commission to guard, protect, and maintain, as well as to work the soil, demonstrates the intimate care with which humans are to relate to the earth. While human occupations would expand to include stock-raising and developing new technology (Genesis 4:20-22), the first occupation in the Bible is that of farming the soil. Furthermore, the relationship of humans to the rest of the creatures, described as "dominion" in Genesis 1, is attested to in the second chapter in terms of the human role of naming and classifying the animals, a highly intellectual task.

It is important to note that human labor and responsibility are founded in the creative work and plan of God. Because such work can result in creation blessings for the worker, a prophet would one day consider labor to be part of God's new creation as well (Isaiah 65:21-23). Thus the promise of food for all God's creatures (Genesis 1:29-30) and the means by which to produce food (occupation) develop eschatological significance as the Bible witnesses to God's creative work.

4) **The relationship of human to human** is limited in the early chapters of Genesis to that between male and female. The content of this relationship is clearly one of equality according to the biblical views of creation. Classic is the little poem in Genesis 1, each line of which is synonymous with the next:

> So God created man in his own image,
>     in the image of God he created him;
>     male and female he created them.

(Genesis 1:27)

When one separates from each line the subject (God, he, he), the direct object (man, him, them), and the identical verb (created), one is left with these words of synonymous meaning: "in his own image," "in the image of God," and "male and female." The poem demonstrates that the image of God consists of both male and female, created simultaneously and equally to have responsible dominion over all other creatures.

While narrating a different sequence of created phenomena, the author of Genesis 2 likewise portrays male and female as equal. According to that story, the male was created first, placed in the garden of Eden to enjoy its pleasures, and then directed to maintain it. But when God observed the man, something was missing: "It is not good that the man should be alone; I will make a helper fit for him" (2:18). Ultimately, this "helper" turned out to be woman. Unfortunately, the traditional translation continued by the **Revised Standard Version** has led to serious misinterpretations in regard to sexuality. A more literal and accurate translation of the phrase quoted above is "a help/strength as his counterpart." Strikingly, the Hebrew word used here for "help" (**RSV**: "helper") is used elsewhere in the Old Testament exclusively in relation to God. The term, therefore, can in no way imply sublimation or inferior status, or even mere assistantship. The author of this story conveys in another way the same relationship between men and women as the later writer of Genesis 1: male and female are created equal by God.

Another aspect of this relationship is sex itself. Already in these first two chapters of Genesis, two aspects of sex are indicated: reproduction and pleasure. In terms of reproduction, the priestly writer of Genesis 1 relates the creation blessing of God to the humans immediately after their creation in God's image: "Be fruitful and multiply, and fill the earth" (1:28). Originally addressed to exiles in danger of dying out as a people in Babylon, these words nevertheless indicate that progeny, and the means by which they are accomplished, are part of God's plan of *shalom* for an orderly world. Just as the trees and plants have the ability to reproduce their own species—and thus contribute to order—so likewise human beings have the ability to propagate themselves. The storyteller of Genesis 2 does not explicitly deal with reproduction as a function of sex until relating the birth of Cain in Genesis 4. What is emphasized earlier is the mutual physical attraction of the sexes who are naked and unashamed, thus attesting to the sexual attraction between the male and the female. In a later writing called The Song of Songs, we find a fuller development of the *shalom* of sexual pleasure.

The four basic relationships outlined here on the basis of Genesis 1 and 2 represent the means by which God exercises divine rule over creation. That rule is one of order and consistency rather than one of anarchy. Yet it is a rule marked by the gift of freedom, particularly for the humans created in God's image and responsible to God for all else. It is a reign in which God provides humanity with the necessities of life: living space, food, occupation, companionship, wisdom, and language. These necessities come as close as anything in the Bible to comprising what we today call "human rights."

People live out their responsibilities in God's world through reason, skill, and labor. In this realm, called by Luther the kingdom on the left, orderliness is maintained through laws and standards by which all are expected to abide. It is human reason by which such guidelines are set and by which skills are measured. Already in the creation stories of Genesis 1 and 2, the function of wisdom—or reason—plays a considerable role. The commission given to male and female that they should "have dominion" assumes that reason will prevail; "dominion" implies a royal education in the reponsibilities of governing and ordering the state of things. Furthermore, when God led the animals before the human "to see what he would call them," a highly intellectual activity was required: that of listing the created beings in terms of genus, species, and the like. Even the task of tilling and keeping the ground involves as much worldly wisdom as it does physical brawn.

## The Disorders of Human Sin

The biblical record continues only as far as Genesis 3 before the humans have broken the trust God placed in them and thereby thrown into conflict all the relationships God had established. The refusal of male and female alike to live with the one prohibition God made, namely, that of eating of "the tree of the knowledge of good and evil," has disastrous results for the whole creation.

**The relationship between God and the world** is affected: the good and blessed ground is "cursed" because of human sin (3:17). No longer is God able to look at the world and announce that it is "good," for the orderly rule has been invaded by the chaos of human sin.

**The relationship of God to humans** is strained because of their disobedience, and so the primary couple is driven from the near presence of God. Distrust and shame, along with guilt and alienation, now appear as the marks of this relationship.

**The relationship between humans and the world** is affected in two ways: first, there would be hostility between humans and animals (particularly snakes) instead of nurturing dominion (3:15), and second, the man would now work the ground in vain (3:17-19) instead of experiencing the fruit of his labor, and both humans would be expelled from the garden of delight.

**The relationship between the sexes** is thrown into conflict as well. To the woman God said, "I will greatly multiply your pain in childbearing; in pain you shall bring forth children, yet your desire shall be for your husband and he shall rule over you." Interestingly, nothing is said of that relationship to the man. But the man suffers here, too. Insofar as the beautiful partnership intended by God was destroyed, then in that relationship the man loses *shalom* as well — wholeness, completeness, is no longer possible.

Some of the effects of this broken relationship between the sexes and the resulting hierarchy appear in Israel's law codes. Clearly, a double standard for women exists in matters of premarital virginity (Genesis 19:8; Deuteronomy 22:20-21), of punishment for infidelity in marriage (Numbers 5:11-31; Deuteronomy 32:22-27), and even of taking a vow (Numbers 30:1-15). In the Decalogue, the classic law code in the Old Testament, the wife is considered along with ox, ass, and servant to be the property which belongs to a man's house (Exodus 20:17).

**The human-to-human relationship** is affected in every way as the story of sin and brokenness continues in the book of Genesis. Cain kills his own brother over an argument that began at the altar of God, and as a result the hostility of humans to one another, even within the same family, is seen to be based in our universal sinfulness.

The brokenness of human relationships in our world is particularly obvious in terms of the ways many people deal with persons of different races. Indeed, racist attitudes and activities—overt as well as subtle—might present the most radical examples of brokenness both in past history and in the present time. Yet, strikingly, the separation of humanity into races is not, according to the biblical witnesses, a matter of God's judgment on sin; racial diversity, on the contrary, is related to God's blessing.

The issue of race, while not discussed explicitly, is alluded to in the story of the sons of Noah, one of whom was Ham, the "father" of Cush, Egypt, Put, and Canaan (Genesis 10:6). The possibility of racial distinctions occurs in the mention of Cush, the Hebrew name for Ethiopia, a land of black people. Moreover, that this family tree follows the story about Ham's seeing the nakedness of his father has contributed to the thinking that the development of races is to be viewed negatively, that is, as judgment against Ham and his offspring.

This traditional interpretation about the "curse" on the descendants of Ham is lacking in several respects. First, the story about Noah's nakedness concludes with a curse on Canaan, not Ham, and, from the point of view of the Hebrew author, that curse is to be understood on the basis of the conflict with Canaanite religion. Second, the story about Noah's nakedness and the genealogy of Noah's son Ham are the work of two different authors. The writer of the former is the same one who told of Adam and Eve in Eden and of the fratricide of Cain against Abel. This author's purpose throughout this portion of the epic (Genesis 3-11) was to explain the brokenness and tensions of the world. The writer of the genealogy, however, wrote to explain that the development of the human race into nations—and, incidentally, into races—was the fulfillment of God's blessing issued first at creation and repeated to Noah: "Be fruitful and multiply, and fill the earth..." (Genesis 1:28; cf. 9:7). Thus, far from being a negative factor in the biblical story, the genealogy regarding races and nations is viewed positively.

Throughout the Bible there are a number of stories which appear to reflect attitudes toward persons of different racial backgrounds. For example, Samson's parents objected to their son's attraction to a Philistine woman (Judges 14), and Abraham insisted that his son not marry a Canaanite woman (Genesis 24). It is difficult to be certain, however, that the issue is racial rather than religious. The Philistines were called the "uncircumcised," for they were not of God's covenant people, Israel, but in fact oppressors of Israel. The Canaanites were worshipers of Baal rather than of the Lord, and their fertility religion constantly seduced Israelites into forsaking the Lord, the God of Israel. The mixing in marriage of Israelites and Canaanites or Philistines presented serious religious difficulties, since Israel was called to be a "holy" (separate) people, devoted to the exclusive worship of God.

On the issue of color, there seems to be only one instance in the Bible where the color of a person's skin presents a problem. Moses' marriage to a Cushite woman (Numbers 12) that causes his brother and sister, Aaron and Miriam, to express their anger, even to the point of challenging Moses' sole leadership of the people. If the woman was indeed Ethiopian (rather than Babylonian, as some manuscripts suggest), then her blackness might have been the issue. In response to this sibling reaction to the mixed marriage, God caused Miriam's hand — ironically — to become "leprous, as white as snow." It seems that, having made an issue out of color, Miriam experienced the unambiguous judgment of God.

Indeed, Ethiopians are mentioned throughout the Bible only in favorable terms. It was an Ethiopian who advocated on behalf of Jeremiah in order to save the prophet from certain death (Jeremiah 38). It was an Ethiopian whom Philip taught and baptized after that man invited the apostle to sit with him and explain the meaning of a scriptural passage (Acts 8:26-40). And, in his prophetic judgments against Israel, the prophet Amos proclaimed that the people of Israel had no exclusive rights to God and God's grace:

> "Are you not like the Ethiopians to me, O people of Israel?"
> says the Lord.

(Amos 9:7)

It is difficult to say whether the authors of these stories intended to emphasize the color of the Ethiopians or simply to allude to their national origin. However, that no issue is made out of color, except perhaps in the story in Numbers 12, should prevent any rationalization of racial prejudice by the use of Scripture. More to the point, any discrimination of one racial group against another or any attempt to exclude on the basis of color runs contrary to the biblical record in terms of creation and redemption.

The diversity of races and colors among humankind is not, then, one of the results of brokenness in creation because of sin. Racial distinction is not a result of the curse of God on the human family, as some have suggested. It is clear that racism is of human origin, and as such it is a particularly monstrous manifestation of human sinfulness. Humans have built into their own systems of values a separation among God's humanity which is completely contrary to God's designs, even in a broken world. Racism is nothing less than the idolatry of one's own race over against the Creator who made all humans in the image of God.

All of the basic relationships which God established in creation have been invaded by the chaos of human sin. Yet that invasion did not remove God from those basic relationships. Even in the act of expelling man and woman from the garden, God demonstrated love and grace for them by providing clothing to keep their bodies warm (Genesis 3:21). Furthermore, by preventing the humans from eating from the tree of immortality, God exercised compassion, for the humans would not be required to live eternally "east of Eden" (Genesis :22-24).

Moreover, even outside the paradise condition, humans would perform their tasks in the world on the basis of their God-given reason. That human wisdom continued, even in the broken creation, is seen most dramatically in the genealogy of Cain (Genesis 4:17-22). The accomplishments of his descendants included the building of cities, the skill of cattle-raising, the development of musical instruments, and the forging of bronze and iron implements. These and similar human skills are highlighted throughout the book of Proverbs and, above all, in a so-called Hymn to Wisdom, while simultaneously the poet reserves to God **the** wisdom which holds the key to the universe (Job 28).

## God's Mission and the Call of Israel

Even after the wickedness and rebellion of the humans, God was willing to deal graciously with them. With the call of Abraham, God began a new means of communicating grace: human mediation. It was to Abraham that God made unconditional promises of a great nation, of blessing and renown. And yet, what is emphasized in the account of this call is not God's benevolence to Abraham, but the function in God's mission Abraham is given: "*so that* you will be a blessing" (Genesis 12:1-2). Those who will experience this blessing through Abraham are not only his own people yet to be established, but "all the families of the land" (12:3).

The historical context for this version of Abraham's call has been identified as the tenth century B.C., the "golden age" of Israel's history. This period was the time of the Davidic-Solomonic Empire when the "great nation" promised to Abraham was realized among the people. In the midst of splendor, affluence, and power, the author (known only as the Yahwist) constructed his history of Israel with two primary goals in mind. First, he needed to remind the people that it was not their own doing but the faithful working of God which brought them to this point in their history. God's promises to Abraham were fulfilled exclusively by God, even without their cooperation. Second, God's promises and intentions for blessing extended far beyond their own people to include "all the families of the land," that is, all those peoples living on the territory of their empire who were not Israelites. The fortunes of the Ammonites, Moabites, Girgashites, Jebusites, and all others in Israel's midst were Israel's responsibility. In one way or another, Israel was to be a source of blessing for all these others so that they might experience the creation blessings of God, rather than the continual curses of brokenness which humanity brought upon itself. The Yahwist developed this theme throughout his history by repeating regularly the formula "by you shall all families of the land be blessed." By placing the formula in the context of well-placed stories, he provided examples of behavior for the

Israel of his own day to follow.

The first example of mediated blessing provided by the Yahwist is one of advocacy. In the story of the visit to Abraham by "three men" (one of whom was apparently God), the Lord revealed to the patriarch the divine judgment about to occur at Sodom and Gomorrah, "seeing that Abraham shall become a great and mighty nation, and all the nations of the earth shall bless themselves by him" (Genesis 18:18). Following the revelation of Sodom's fate is one of the most profound discussions between God and humans in the entire Bible. Abraham plays his role as a mediator of blessing by persistent intercession on behalf of the inhabitants of the doomed city. Abraham's access to the ears of God gives him the responsibility of speaking for those in Sodom who lacked the knowledge or the opportunity to speak for themselves. Because of Abraham's advocacy, if only ten righteous people had been found there, the city would not have been destroyed (18:32). The message for Israel of the tenth century B.C. was that Israel had been chosen by God to restore creation harmony through such advocacy and other means. Failing that task because of the sin common to all humanity, Israel eventually looked for this restoration in God's kingdom to come "on that day" about which the prophets spoke.

# CHAPTER 2

# The Kingdom Promised and Fulfilled

The confession that the Lord was Israel's King first appears in the story about God's victory at the sea (Exodus 15:18). That the Lord remained Israel's King even in the Davidic-Solomonic monarchy is evident in many scriptural passages. However, when that political kingdom split, it was not obvious that God's rule over Israel was intact. Disorder seemed to prevail over God's order. One of the results was the development of a future hope that God would be victorious over forces hostile to the divine orderly rule, and that God would reestablish the divine reign unambiguously and forever.

## Prophetic Vision: The Opposite of What Is Seen

In the Scriptures, particularly in the preaching of ancient Israel's prophets, "the last days," or such similar expressions as "on that day" or "in those days" were formulas which introduced some message about the coming reign of God. "The day of the Lord" was the time in which God would make a divine claim on the world, and thus begin a new and universal reign over people everywhere. Such prophecies envisioned a new time in which the brokenness of life would be restored. In a sense, these prophetic

15

visions promised the opposite of what people were seeing and experiencing in their present situations.

Those visions of a new time promise, among other things, the transformation of the four basic relationships. **The relationship between God and the world**, so "good" at the time of creation, but cursed by the sin of humanity, will be restored so dramatically that in the days to come "the plowman shall overtake the reaper and the treader of grapes him who sows the seed; the mountains shall drip with sweet wine, and the hills shall flow with it" (Amos 9:13).

**The relationship between God and people**, so intimate at creation, but marked by shame, guilt, and alienation because of sin, will be changed by the gift to humanity of a new heart. The result will be that "I will be their God, and they shall be my people ...they shall all know me from the least of them to the greatest" (Jeremiah 31:33-34). In that new time to come, not only Israel, but all peoples will flow to Mount Zion to learn the law of the Lord (Isaiah 2:2-4; Micah 4:1-3).

As for **the relationship between humans and the world**, Isaiah prophesied that the new day will be a time of such harmony among all creatures that even wolves and lambs will dwell together, and all animals presently hostile to one another will feed together; even children and snakes will live in such peace that one will not hurt the other—quite the opposite of the situation which has prevailed since the curse of sin in Eden's garden (see Isaiah 11:6-9). The new heaven and new earth will be a time when work will be done as it was in Eden, before the "toil" of Genesis 3; humans will "not labor in vain," but live in the houses they build and eat the produce of their gardens (Isaiah 65:17-25).

**The relationship between humans and humans** will be restored as a result of the reconciliation of humans to God. On that new day when all nations will come to Mount Zion to learn the will and law of the Lord, such a pilgrimage will result in the recycling of the instruments of war into agricultural tools (Isaiah 2:2-4; also Micah 4:1-3). Further, the sexual hierarchy which resulted from sin will be leveled when the spirit of God, poured out in those days on all flesh, will lead to prophecy by men and women alike, and by people of all ages and stations of life. Such equality is to be restored over no less an issue than preaching the word of God (Joel 2:28-29).

The signs of the kingdom to come extend beyond even these basic relationships to include other transformations as well. A prophet we know only as Second Isaiah prophesied that the homecoming of Jerusalem's exiles from Babylon would mark the coming reign of God (Isaiah 52:7-10). That return would be accompanied by the transformation of human frailties to human prowess: weak hands will be strengthened, feeble knees made firm, the blind will see, the lame walk, and the mute speak (Isaiah 35).

However, when the exiles did indeed return to Jerusalem, they experienced nothing of the expected transformations; instead, they encountered pain, alienation, and disillusionment. And so another prophet was anointed by God's Spirit to announce that the signs of the kingdom were yet to come: the poor will have good news preached to them, the brokenhearted will be bound up, the captives will hear the proclamation of liberty, and those who mourn will be comforted (Isaiah 61:1-2).

That the future kingdom of God is to be a time of good news for the oppressed and the outcast is the theme of several other prophets. Far from being marked by their sufferings as the scourge of God (as according to some proverbial traditions), the afflicted would make up the remnant, a strong nation over whom God will rule on Mount Zion (Micah 4:6-7; Zephaniah 3:18-19).

Such were some of the expectations connected with the "day of the Lord," when God would usher in that unambiguous reign over all creation. God's intentions for relationships, so harmonious at the time of creation but rendered discordant by human sin, will be restored through God's act of reconciliation.

## The Inbreaking of the Kingdom

The gospels are clear in their assertion that the kingdom of God was being realized in the ministry, death, and resurrection of Jesus. Indeed, the earliest gospel, that according to Mark, summarizes the preaching of Jesus as the gospel of God: "The time is fulfilled; the kingdom of God is at hand; repent and believe in the gospel" (Mark 1:15). Matthew follows a similar presentation of Jesus' initial preaching, while Luke presents a dramatic picture about Jesus' appearance in his hometown synagogue at Nazareth.

On that occasion, Jesus read the prophecy from Isaiah 61:1-2 about the poor having good news preached to them. When Jesus had finished reading the text, he delivered a one-sentence sermon: "Today this scripture has been fulfilled in your hearing" (Luke 4:21). The announcement meant that the time for the awaited eschatological reversals was occurring in the ministry of Jesus.

Both Matthew and Luke continue that same theme in their story in which John sends his disciples to ask whether Jesus is "he who is to come." Jesus' response indicated that the signs of the expected kingdom were taking place in his ministry:

> "The blind receive their sight, the lame walk, lepers are cleansed, and the deaf hear, the dead are raised up, the poor have good news preached to them."

(Luke 7:22; Matthew 11:4)

While Jesus taught on many occasions that his own death and resurrection were necessary in fulfilling Old Testament prophecy (e.g., Luke 24:46), it was the apostle Paul who directly related this to the eschatological event. According to Luke's record of Paul's preaching, the apostle explained and proved "that it was necessary for the Christ to suffer and to rise from the dead" according to the Hebrew Scriptures (see Acts 17:2-3). Furthermore, Paul's reference to Christ's resurrection as "the first fruits of those who have fallen asleep" (1 Corinthians 15:20) is his way of indicating that the kingdom has already dawned. It was also Paul who argued that since "the day is at hand," those who belong to "the day" have an ethical responsibility to demonstrate in word and deed the reality of the new age (Romans 13:11-14).

This dawning of the kingdom and its realization as a new people on earth brings with it other effects, including a reversal of situations permeating the world since the sin of Adam and Eve. Indeed, the four relationships defined at creation are already being restored as signs that the new time has begun.

**The relationship between God and humans** is the major issue in the New Testament witnesses. That which God accomplished on the cross of Christ is the act of justification, God's declaration that, while all have sinned and keep falling short of the glory of God, all are free to belong to God (Romans 3:21-26). Whether one emphasizes justification, redemption, atonement, expiation, or righteousness—all are images or analogies to announce God's forgiveness of human sin by which the relationship intended at the creation is restored. As a result of this reconciling act, we are once again on intimate terms with our Creator, even enabled to call God by the familial "*Abba*," rather than the formal term "Father."

Indeed, even **the relationship between God and the world** is reconciled by God in Christ (2 Corinthians 5:19), for "God so loved the world that he gave his only begotten son" (John 3:16). It would appear that God sent Christ to the cross for all of creation, even though the world does not recognize what God has done and will remain in its brokenness until Christ comes again.

The restoration of the **human to human relationship** is demonstrated in several ways. As a sign of the new age, Paul pointed to the reality of Jews and Gentiles as one worshiping community in Rome; using passages from Scripture, he demonstrated that the eschatological miracle was occurring in that congregation's praise of God (Romans 15:7-13). Here is the fulfillment of the hope that the human-human relationship would be restored on the basis of common worship (Isaiah 2:2-4). In addition, Paul indicates—contrary to the curse of Genesis 3:16, according to which the husband would rule over the wife—that on the issue of conjugal rights, male and female rule each other's bodies in reciprocal fashion (1 Corinthians 7:4). There is also Paul's rather convoluted argument regarding the need for women to cover their heads in worship, an argumentation based, it seems, on Greek custom. In the midst of it all, Paul states the new, distinctly Christian understanding: the interdependence of male and female "in the Lord" (1 Corinthians 11:11). Finally, Paul's classic expression regarding the impotence of earthly distinctions appears in his Epistle to the Galatians: "There is neither Jew nor Greek, there is neither slave nor free, there is neither male nor female; for you are all one in Christ Jesus" (Galatians 3:28).

These powerful passages about the restoration of sexual equality balance some others in the New Testament—even in Paul's writings—which suggest that Paul had not fully comprehended the newness of the situation, that he was still caught up in the struggle with the prevailing culture. In this light, it seems, we are to understand his admonition that women are to keep silent in the church (1 Corinthians 12:33a-36), if indeed these verses belong to Paul's own hand. Furthermore, there is the often cited instruction that "wives, be subject to your husbands" (Ephesians 5:22). It needs to be said in this case, however, that the mutuality of responsibility between husband and wife occurs only a few verses later, when Paul admonishes husbands to "love your wives, as

Christ loved the church and gave himself up for her'' (Ephesians 5:25).

To conclude: when the New Testament writers bore their witness to the act of God in Christ, they saw the restoration of creation's relationships beginning in his ministry, death, and resurrection. This restoration was not identical to the original creation, however, for now all things are reconciled through Christ. With the risen and exalted Lord now present in all relationships, there is a new element in this new creation: Jesus is Lord over all as co-regent with the Father.

Apparently quoting already established creeds and hymns, Paul on several occasions relates Christ to creation. One such example occurs in his discussion regarding food offered to idols:

> Yet for us there is one God, the Father, from whom are all things and from whom we exist, and one Lord, Jesus Christ, through whom are all things and through whom we exist.
>
> (1 Corinthians 8:6)

Even more pronounced is the two-stanza hymn regarding the role of the "beloved Son" in creation and in reconciliation of the universe: "All things were created through him and for him..., and through him to reconcile to himself all things whether on earth or in heaven, making peace by the blood of the cross" (Colossians 1:15-20).

Yet, simultaneously, the church can recognize that the same exalted Lord is the Incarnate One who knew the depths of human pain and suffering, who became so involved "in the world" that he gave his own life for its sake, whose body and blood are the gifts of God to the broken world.

## "Thy Kingdom Come"

Even while the New Testament witnesses testify to the Christian church as the work accomplished in Christ, they simultaneously point to another event—still in the future—in which the kingdom of God will be fully consummated. One of the ways in which the early Christian writers dealt with this future reign—while simultaneously proclaiming its presence now—was to speak of two reigns. Paul distinguishes between the present time and the future in terms of the reign of Christ now and the kingdom of God the Father to come. Christ will reign until "he has put all his enemies under his feet; then he will deliver the kingdom to the Father" (1 Corinthians 15:24). Likewise, according to Matthew's Gospel, Jesus teaches in a parable that the kingdom of the Son of Man will precede the kingdom of the Father (Matthew 13:37-43).

Another way in which the gospels distinguish a future event from the present is by the use of different groups of sayings about the "Son of Man." Placed on the lips of Jesus, one group of Son of Man sayings speaks of a future Son of Man, seated at the right hand of God, who will come on the clouds of heaven to manifest glory (e.g., Matthew 26:64). These sayings contrast with another group of Son of Man sayings which point to Jesus during the time of his earthly ministry (e.g., Mark 8:31).

In still another way, Paul makes explicit the distinction between the two times. The apostle speaks of the present time as the one in which we have received justification, and thus peace with God. This present gift is contrasted with the hope of the future when we shall also be saved from the wrath of God (Romans 5:1-9). According to this reasoning, we live now with the gift of justification and, simultaneously, with the hope of salvation to come in the future.

This future event will be a time when Christ will come again, this time in glory; when the dead in Christ will be raised to eternal life; when—to use apocalyptic terms—the chaos of the sea, of death and mourning will be no more, and the tree of life will stand on the riverside, full of leaves "for the healing of the nations"

(Revelation 22:2). Such is the vision of the glorious reign to come with which the Bible ends.

Therefore, the Christian exists in two times simultaneously: the time of the new day insofar as the "communion of saints" exists as the sign of God's reign, and the time of the night when pain and hopelessness, death and mourning, war and disharmony continue. This dual time is for the church a time of joy and harmony but, simultaneously, a time of discord and pain. Even when this community called the church experiences itself in its visible form, that is, gathered for worship as a body, it is obvious that the will of God is not complete, that the reign of God is not fully realized. For in its own body and in the world there remains the darkness of the former time. In that darkness live hunger, pain, racism, sexism, injustice, abuse of women and children, manipulation of the powerful over the powerless, loneliness, frustration, fear, uncertainty, and vulnerability.

This dual existence forces the Christian and the Christian communion to struggle with an understanding of a proper **relationship to the world**. Traditionally, Christians are said to be "in but not of the world." Such an awareness is derived from the scriptural testimony regarding the realm to which we belong. As Paul put it, "Our commonwealth is in heaven, and from it we await a Savior, the Lord Jesus Christ" (Philippians 3:20). The author of 1 Peter develops the same theme in terms of identity and witness in a non-Christian environment. That letter is addressed "to the exiles of the Dispersion" (1 Peter 1:1), who are exhorted to "conduct yourselves with fear during the time of your exile" (1:17). The audience is further besought "as aliens and exiles to abstain from the passions of the flesh that wage war against your soul" (2:11). That these "aliens and exiles" are Christians is explained on the basis of their baptism: "By his great mercy we have been born anew to a living hope through the resurrection of Jesus Christ from the dead" (1:3). In other words, physical birth from the mother's womb makes one a citizen of the world, but being born anew through baptism defines one as a child of God's new kingdom but as an alien in the world.

Clearly, the Christian is not taken out of the world, but remains in it as an exile whose "commonwealth is in heaven." Such an existence is integral to the tension between the present and future reign of God, and it is in the tension of these two times that the church participates in God's mission.

# CHAPTER 3

# God's Mission Under the Cross

## The Church in the In-Between Time

Although the Christian church is the sign of the end time, the church may never consider itself the end of God's concern, but, rather, the means by which God reaches out to the world. While joining the world in longing for an end to discord and suffering, the church is called by God to proclaim the good news of the kingdom and to serve the world in its present suffering. This proclamation and service lies at the heart of the word "mission": "sent" by God to serve the world on God's behalf.

The biblical understanding of Christ provides the church with a perspective on its role in God's mission. The Risen Lord who sits at the right hand of God and serves as co-regent with the Father is none other than the Incarnate One who knew the depths of human misery and pain, who became so involved in the world that he gave his life for its sake, and whose body and blood are the gifts of God to the broken world. Confession of faith in that Crucified Lord cannot be separated from involvement in and service to the world. Broken as the world is, we in the church are called to continue Christ's work to the glory of God.

Instructive for the way the church relates to the world is the structure of Paul's letter to the Romans. The first eleven chapters of the epistle develop in systematic terms the meaning of justification as God's free and gracious gift for all humankind, Jew and Gentile alike. The eleventh chapter ends with hymnic praise about the unfathomable nature of God. Then, with chapter 12, Paul begins the so-called ethical section of the letter, clearly based on all that precedes:

> I appeal to you therefore, brethren, by the mercies of God, to present your bodies as a living sacrifice, holy and acceptable to God, which is your spiritual worship. Do not be conformed to this world but be transformed by the renewal of your mind, that you may prove what is the will of God, what is good and acceptable and perfect.

> (Romans 12:1-2)

Paul's exhortation to the Romans, asking them to present their bodies as a living sacrifice, understood to be "spiritual/rational worship," clearly prohibits Christians from withdrawing from the world. On the contrary, that such an exhortation begins the section dealing with governing authorities, taxes, financial obligations, food, days, and the poor in Jerusalem attests to an incarnational involvement in the world. Christianity is, therefore, not a private matter, but a public one. Justification does not isolate us from one another, but brings us together with all people with whom we share the blessings of God. In and through the gospel, God claims our whole selves—our bodies, our minds, our spirits—individually and corporately, and God does so in order to send us back into the world.

At the same time, this exhortation to worldly involvement is conditioned by Paul's instruction to avoid conforming to the world ("not of the world"). The world remains as that totality which—because of human sin—stands over against God, and thus is always subject to its own will rather than to that of the Creator. Insofar as this world is opposed to God, it cannot set the agenda for the church. Instead, Paul exhorts the church to be "transformed by the renewal of your mind." What seems to distinguish the Christian from the world is a different type of thinking, a new wisdom, a new mind. While Paul does not define the thought more precisely in this place, several of his other letters give some indication of what is meant by this "renewed mind." In his Corinthian correspondence, Paul attacks the wisdom of this world for its presumption to know God. God's wisdom, on the contrary, is precisely what the world considers t be foolish: the crucifixion of Jesus Christ (1 Corinthians 1:18-25). As he develops this theme, Paul further distinguishes worldly wisdom from God's:

> Yet among the mature we do impart wisdom, although it is not a wisdom of this age or of the rulers of this age, who are doomed to pass away. But we impart a secret and hidden wisdom of God, which God decreed before the ages for our glorification. None of the rulers of this age understood this; for if they had, they would not have crucified the Lord of glory.

(1 Corinthians 2:6-8)

Another passage which gives some insight into the meaning of the "renewed mind" is the pre-Pauline hymn and its introduction in the second chapter of Paul's letter to the Philippians. Having explained to his audience that it is necessary not only to believe in Christ, but also to suffer for his sake, Paul encourages the Christians in Philippi to be of one mind. Exhorting them to do nothing out of conceit or self-interest, the apostle continues:

> Have this mind among yourselves, which you have in Christ Jesus. (Philippians 2:5)

Then follows the hymn regarding the humiliation of Christ, who "became obedient unto death, even death on a cross" (2:8), which culminates in the exaltation of Christ and his acclamation by the universe. This connection between the "mind...which you have in Christ Jesus" and his death by crucifixion as the supreme example of humility seems quite consistent with the understanding of wisdom as "Christ crucified" in 1 Corinthians. If these two passages from different Pauline epistles can be used to shed light on the "renewal of your mind" in Romans 12:2, then it seems that the new mind is one based upon the transforming power of the crucified Christ.

That vision requires the Christian not to replace wisdom with piety, but to seek a deeper perspective concerning the world, a wisdom which provides Christians with the means to live in the world and serve it on behalf of God. In his letter to the Colossians, the apostle speaks of warning and teaching others "in all wisdom" in order to bring people to maturity (1:28); furthermore, he exhorts the Christians there to "conduct yourselves wisely toward outsiders" (4:5).

Throughout his correspondence to the churches, Paul uses some rather sophisticated arguments, some derived from various schools of philosophy, in order to help them comprehend the meaning of their faith and their roles in the world. Surely Paul does not urge the surrender of reason and logic or the skills for labor, even though he expects Christians to have different insights and ꞏrenewed minds on the basis of the gospel.

Such a distinction between the usefulness of wisdom in creation and its impotence in regard to knowing God or God's mind has something of a parallel in the Augsburg Confession, Article XVIII, concerning freedom of the will:

> It is also taught among us that man possesses some measure of freedom of the will which enables him to live an outwardly honorable life and to make choices among the things that reason comprehends. But without the grace, help, and activity of the Holy Spirit man is not capable of making himself acceptable to God, of fearing God and believing in God with his whole heart, or of expelling inborn evil lusts from his heart (Tappert, p. 39, 1-2 ).

As the discussion continues, those choices made on the basis of reason include laboring, eating and drinking, visiting a friend, dressing, building a house, marrying, engaging in a trade, or any number of "good and profitable" things.

These insights from the Bible and from the Lutheran Confessions are consistent in their understanding that human wisdom plays no role in justification, but contributes to responsible stewardship of daily life in the realm of creation. The Christian and the church cannot ignore the world or escape the tasks given by the Creator; likewise, the church can in no way escape the necessity for worldly wisdom and for promoting the increase of wisdom through education as a task assigned by God to all creatures made in God's image.

## The Vision of the Cross as Strategy for Ministry

While the Christian church serves as a sign of the *eschaton* and thus functions with a vision of the glorious reign of God over creation, the church simultaneously is informed by a vision and communicates a theology of the cross. Even in its recognition of its role as the communion of the end time, the Christian community of Corinth was exhorted by Paul to participate in the Lord's Supper in such a way that they "proclaim the Lord's death until he comes" (1 Corinthians 11:26). In other words, the cross is the focus of proclamation, the very content of word and sacrament, which establishes the norm for the faith and worship of the church.

The same cross provided the basis for Paul's ministry as he worked among the Corinthians. Strikingly, his strategy for ministry among the intellectuals and cosmopolitans of his day was vulnerability:

> When I came to you, brethren, I did not come proclaiming to you the testimony of God in lofty words or wisdom. For I decided to know nothing among you except Jesus Christ and

him crucified. And I was with you in weakness and in much fear and trembling; and my speech and my message were not in plausible words of wisdom, but in demonstration of the Spirit and power, that your faith might not rest in the wisdom of men but in the power of God.

(1 Corinthians 2:1-5)

The vision of the cross by which ministry is to be carried out is one which is marked by weakness, fear, and trembling, and is based on nothing other than "Jesus Christ and him crucified." This approach is the same one Paul commends to the Roman Christians when he exhorts them to "be transformed by the renewal of your mind."

That same vision is what later led Luther to distinguish so sharply between a theology of glory and a theology of the cross:

> The theology of glory seeks to know God directly in his obviously divine power, wisdom, and glory; whereas the theology of the cross paradoxically recognizes him precisely where he has hidden himself, in his sufferings and in all that which the theology of glory considers to be weakness and foolishness. (Paul Althaus, **The Theology of Martin Luther**, trans. Robert C. Schultz [Philadelphia: Fortress Press], 1966, p. 27.)

Such a theology of the cross permeated all Luther's thinking and led, in fact, to a proper understanding of reality. Reality is not what the world sees, but, like the Old Testament prophecies about the kingdom of God to come "on that day," the reality of God is hidden. Such is the understanding of faith: while enduring the contradictions of sight, reason, and experience (the means by which the world judges reality), faith must be based solely on God's word of promise. Faith in that promise prohibits the church from avoiding the reality of human existence, which is the experience of trouble, weakness, and death. Indeed, in repeated descents into that darkness the church finds the reality of God.

Such descents into human need and despair lead to a recognition of the relationship between the theology of the cross and a "theology of place." Throughout both testaments, various spaces serve specific functions in the economy of God. That which is called "the mountain" or "the mountain of God," even "the holy mountain," is the space which marks the presence of God in visible ways. It is to the mountain that God invites certain individuals and groups, there reveals the divine identity and that of Christ, provides for eating and drinking together in the divine presence, issues the law, and commissions certain people to be agents of the divine will and apostles of the kingdom (Exodus 3:1-15; 24:9-11; Luke 6:12-15; Mark 9:2-9).

It is above all in Luke that such theological geography centers on another space: "the place" (Greek *topos*). In contrast to "the mountain," to which special persons are invited, "the place" is that space where Jesus seeks solitude, but is besought by others and disturbed. These disturbances are always welcomed by Jesus as providing opportunities to teach (Luke 4:42; 6:17; 11:1), to feed the multitudes (Luke 9:12-17), and to heal those who had need to be cured (Luke 6:18; 9:11). That "the place" is the space where public ministry occurs serves to focus on the designation in all four gospels of the site of the crucifixion: "the place" which is called Golgotha. The greatest act of public ministry occurred there: Christ died for the sins of humanity. "The place" is, in other words, the space in which the theology of the cross comes to clear expression: where weakness, doubt, contradiction, limitation, sacrifice, and service all occur as the means by which God reaches out to the world.

If Jesus' ministry can serve as the model for the church's participation in God's mission ("Have this mind among yourselves, which you have in Christ Jesus"), then the church must keep in proper tension its life "on the mountain" and its role "in the place." The functions of "the mountain" described above are most readily accomplished for the church in its corporate worship. There, as it gathers, the church hears the news of and about God through the proclamation of the cross; there it eats and drinks as a community of sisters and brothers; there the priesthood of all believers is commissioned to serve the needy neighbor; there it comes to know the identity of God and of Jesus Christ in ways which are incomprehensible to the world. There, in other words, the assembled family is nourished.

Yet, like Jesus and the commissioned apostles, the church must repeatedly "go downhill" into the human condition, must itself experience doubt and fear, and must reach out to those who know only the darkness of human existence and the forsakenness of God. Furthermore, like Jesus, the church enters such darkness, not with an air of hostility, but with an atmosphere of hospitality; not with an impression that it has all the answers, but with a willingness to admit it shares in the questions; not with restricting programs, but with an openness to learn and respond to genuine needs. (For a more comprehensive treatment of the functions of "the mountain" and "the place," see Foster R. McCurley, **Ancient Myths and Biblical Faith** [Philadelphia: Fortress Press, 1984], pp. 126-182, 188-190.)

The church at every level of organization needs to examine "the place" in which it is accountable to God's mission. For wherever the church exists and in whatever form, there it encounters "the place" which is marked by human need, expressing itself in spiritual and physical hunger, in alienation and brokenness, in injustice and manipulation. Just as the church takes many forms, so does "the place" vary in terms of its constituency. For local congregations or for a coalition of congregations, "the place" is the community in which they are located. For a synod, it might be a section of a state or group of states covering a wide geographical territory. "The place" for the churchwide agencies is the United States, or even the world itself. Each such "place" has its agenda determined by the needs of human beings, and in each such "place" the church offers the hospitality of its service.

Whatever the expanse of "the place," however, the interdependence rather than the independence of the institution's parts is vital for God's mission. Each such institutional part has resources and forms of expertise which contribute to effective ministry to people in need.

This understanding of "place" as the space in which the church and its members encounter human need runs counter to any attempt to sacralize a particular space. To do so is nothing short of idolatry. Rather, the "place" is every space where the church meets people in order to minister to their individual and collective needs. It is also that space where the church is nourished, for in its ministry *alongside* the needy of the world, the church finds the reality of the crucified Christ. Yet at the center of all the church's involvement at "the place" is the proclamation of the word of God.

# CHAPTER 4

# The Church's Outreach Through Word and Sacrament

The local congregation consisting of pastor and people is the focus of the ministry of word and sacrament. Whatever the meeting space, the functions of "the mountain" are crucial for whatever else the congregation does. There the congregation speaks and hears the word of God, sings praises to the Triune Deity, and teaches the meaning of its existence to all people. There it is nurtured and continues to nurture itself through the proclamation of the gospel and administration of the sacraments in accord with that gospel.

This word of God which sends out the church and which the church is called to proclaim is not a set of dogmatic principles or a memorized speech, but a dynamic encounter between God and humans which is never repeated in precisely the same way. In the Old Testament the expression "the word of the Lord" occurs more than two hundred times, always resulting in speeches which differ from one another. Particularly common is the prophetic formula "the word of the Lord came to ...." What follows that expression are the words and will of God which the prophets were to speak to Israel in different times and places.

This dynamic diversity of God's expression of will and action for Israel, and ultimately for all people, demonstrates that the word is always directed to the changing situations which people experience. This characteristic of God's word cannot be overstated: in the word God meets people in ways which are relevant to the needs of the moment.

In his "Preface to the Prophets," Martin Luther stressed the necessity of understanding the word in its relationship to historical and sociological situations:

> For if one would understand the prophecies, it is necessary that one know how things were in the land, how matters lay, what was in the mind of the people—what plans they had with respect to their neighbors, friends, and enemies—and especially what attitude they took in their country toward God and toward the prophet, whether they held to his word and worship or to idolatry. (E. Theodore Bachmann, ed., **Word and Sacrament I**, vol. 35 of **Luther's Works**, Helmut T. Lehmann, ed. [Philadelphia: Fortress Press, 1960], p. 274.)

A few examples from the Bible will suffice to support this approach. At Hosea 1:2-3 the Lord commands the prophet to take "a wife of harlotry and have children of harlotry" (**RSV**). In seemingly contradictory fashion, the same Lord exhorts the prophet Jeremiah not to marry or have children (Jeremiah 16:1-2). How are we to understand these contradictory commands on the basis of "how matters lay in the land"? According to the superscription of Hosea, we can conclude that the prophet preached in the northern kingdom of Israel during the second half of the eighth century B.C. It is clear from this prophet's preaching as well as elsewhere that the rich, lush territory known later as Galilee was the hotbed of Canaanite fertility religion. This seductive religion managed to lure into its devotion and practice many of the Israelites who had been called to worship the Lord exclusively. Hosea's purpose (and that of his predecessor, Elijah) was to call the people back to the God who had delivered them from Egypt. The means which God chose for Hosea's task was marriage to an Israelite woman who had participated in the fashionable Canaanite rites of initiation in order to ensure fertility for a would-be husband. Marriage to such a woman, who represented Israel's infidelity to the Lord, would provide the means for Hosea's proclamation of God's unfailing love for Israel.

The prohibition to Jeremiah, however, occurred at the end of the seventh century B.C. in the city of Jerusalem, capital of Judah. Because of constant rebellion over the years, Judah was about to be devastated by the Lord by means of the Babylonian army of Nebuchadnezzar. The city of Jerusalem would not be a place to begin a family, for nothing but destruction would be its immediate future. Thus the word of God to Jeremiah in Jerusalem was different from the word which he addressed to Hosea almost a century and a half earlier in Israel. "Matters in the land" had changed, and so also did the Lord's word to a prophet.

In the New Testament as well, it is clear that different times, communities, and purposes provide the background for understanding diverse expressions of the word. The synoptic gospels offer ample illustrations of the situation affecting the proclamation of the word. To cite one example, Christ's teaching of the Lord's Prayer has a different thrust in Matthew's Gospel when compared to the version in Luke's. Addressing an essentially Jewish Christian community, Matthew reports Jesus' instructions to his disciples in terms of *how* they should pray in contrast to Gentiles: "Pray then like this..." (Matt. 6:7ff.). On the other hand, Luke's audience, consisting essentially of Gentile Christians apparently unfamiliar with praying, can identify with the plea of one of the disciples, "Lord, teach us to pray, as John taught his disciples." And he said to them, "When you pray, say..." (Luke 11:1ff.).

Indeed, God's word is so directly related to each situation that one must speak of the biblical faith as a constant dialogue between the Lord and the people, rather than as a monologue by some uninvolved deity. In fact, apart from dialogue, one cannot really speak of the God of the Bible. The witnesses of Scripture are not concerned with describing God apart from the dialogical relationship which exists between Israel and God, humanity and God, or the church and God. God is known only in relationship with those who witness in faith to what God says and does. Likewise, one cannot speak of the people of God—Israel or the church—apart from the God who called that people into being. This relationship is constant throughout the Bible, although it changes in form depending on various circumstances.

Dialogue, of course, never takes place in a vacuum. The divine word and human words take form in light of the situations in which people live and on the basis of the relationships in which they are involved with one another and with God. Israel is addressed in a way different from other peoples because "you only have I known of all families of the earth" (Amos 3:2). Only Israel can be sued for divorce by the aggrieved husband, the Lord (Hosea 2:1-13). Even the choice of imagery by these prophets, that is, even the selection of words, is directly related to the husband-wife or the parent-child relationship between the Lord and Israel, a relationship known by some authors as a "covenant."

Words themselves are, of course, human creations, and words have meaning within particular cultural contexts. When the Old Testament speaks of God as "Redeemer," the Hebrew word behind this term reflects that ancient cultural phenomenon in which the next of kin settled matters on behalf of his clan: he would pay damages so that a kinsman might go free, or he would take vengeance on another clan that had deprived his own of a member. In either case, the notion that the Lord served as Israel's "Redeemer" meant something in terms of their relationship with each other, and also promised what the people could expect of their nearest "kin." The word which is translated "redemption" in the New Testament derives from a totally different cultural context; it describes the emancipation of a slave by a particular economic process.

The Hebrew traditions spoke of the Lord's "atonement" by which sins that prevented fellowship between God and the people were removed. This term, derived from Israel's cultic life, did not fit the need at a later time when the apostle Paul carried the message about Jesus Christ to the Gentile world.

This different cultural setting—essentially Greek in thought rather than Hebraic—demanded new words and images in order to communicate what God had accomplished in Jesus Christ. Thus "reconciliation" and a new understanding of "redemption" based not on the act of a next of kin, but on a process of emancipating slaves, were added to the biblical vocabulary.

In addition to vocabulary, different issues were raised in that cultural setting of the Gentile world, and so the gospel took on new forms while simultaneously remaining true to what God had accomplished in Christ.

Such a relationship between culturally laden human words and the word of God raises the question about the extent to which they can be separated. Recognizing the limitations of human communication, some interpreters speak of the Bible as that which "contains" the word of God. The human words are accepted, but somehow God's word is in the midst of them all. The result is a scavenger hunt which attempts to separate the sacred and eternal from the profane and limited. Such a separation—perhaps even merely such a distinction—is theologically problematic, for God demonstrates throughout the Bible, particularly in the Incarnation, the will to use the finite precisely in order to proclaim the Infinite. There is no word of God to humans apart from the words and other symbols by which humans communicate and which they understand. Thus, rather than saying that the Bible contains the word of God, the Reformation tradition drives us to speak of the Bible *as* the word of God in written form.

If the word of God is so indissolubly bound up with the many human words which comprise the Bible, then we are at a loss to select a few as those which adequately define the word. Even the popular John 3:16 cannot by itself limit the word to the extent that the rest of the Bible's syllables are superfluous. In that passage a particular set of human words proclaims God's word, but much more is to be said. In fact, because of the changing circumstances of human life, the word takes so many diverse forms that finally, it is necessary to say that God's word is nothing less than God meeting people to judge and to save, to create and to destroy, to comfort and to afflict.

Such is the nature of the word with which the church is sent to the world of our day to participate in God's mission. That word, dynamic and changing yet consistent with the norm of Holy Scripture, provides the content and the motivation for our outreach to others. This dynamic quality of the word presents a serious challenge to the church, a challenge which requires the full utilization of all the church's resources in order to comprehend both the normative stance of the Bible and also the human or worldly context to which, in which, and through which the word is to be proclaimed.

In order to ensure that this constituting and definitive function of the church occurs, institutional forms of the church need to provide for its proclamation. Such provision involves, of course, the basic education of those called to the ordained ministry according to the standards established for such an "office." But beyond that basic preparation of clergy, the church needs to take responsibility for equipping the laity for their role as the priesthood of all believers, and for the continuing education of clergy and other church professionals.

The good news of the gospel is "the power of God for salvation to every one who has faith" (Romans 1:16). Yet, as we have seen in our study of Holy Scripture, the good news is more than a change in an individual's status before God; it is the announcement to the world that the kingdom of God is at hand. It is a corporate matter as well as an individual one. As such, it is essential for its proclamation that fellowship or communion be the context for its preaching and teaching. It is thus imperative that the church provide the means and the opportunities for its reception.

In order to provide for that reception, various institutional forms of the church need to be involved in the process of selecting new sites for church extension, of reviewing other sites which ought no longer be maintained because of limited resources, or of determining which congregations need further development. Such logistical decisions are founded on the basis of reason and wisdom, gifts from God to humanity at the time of creation. Among such criteria are trends regarding population growth and movement gathered through demographic studies, information gleaned from lending institutions and building contractors concerning the locations of prospective communities, and advice from economists regarding the financial trends of particular communities. However, these reasonable decisions are made by a community of persons representing various constituent parts of the church. Such persons must process worldly data with a "renewed mind," daring at times to act in ways which the world regards as unwise or risky, for such is the way of the cross.

The same dual criteria of worldly wisdom and "renewed mind" serve the church in determining architectural designs for new buildings or the renovation of established ones. In this day buildings designed for congregational life must be energy-efficient, contain rooms that are multi-functional, provide access for handicapped persons, and be cost-efficient in terms of construction and maintenance. However, at the same time, these criteria need to serve the essential function of the church building: to be a space in which an assembly of persons, a congregation, worships God. That space needs to evoke a devotional response and a sense of its purpose for being, namely, the proclamation of the gospel and the administration of the sacraments. Indeed, church architects might consider ways in which the functions of "the mountain" and those of "the place" might be enhanced by the very appearance and structure of the building. If form indeed follows function, then the church must be clear on the functions it needs to accomplish in order to be the church.

Behind its commitment to professional development, selection of sites for church extension, and the architectural possibilities to enhance the functions of the mountain and the place is the church's understanding that every person stands in need of the gospel message. Biblical theology, particularly in the letters of Paul, understands all to "have sinned, continually falling short of the glory of God" (Romans 3:23). Thus all need to hear the message of justification, that unique contribution which the church offers humankind.

In the "place" where we live, the United States of America, there are an estimated 93,000,000 people who are not connected to church or synagogue. Perhaps more astonishing is the estimate that out of a population of 230,000,000, only about 70,000,000 are active in church or synagogue. Thus, in addition to the totally unchurched, there are millions more for whom religious meaning and commitment are absent. To put the matter differently, less than one-third of the population of the United States seems to regard religion as a significant part of their lives.

The challenge these statistics present to the church is enormous indeed. Yet to reach out in word and sacrament to people, indeed, to be effective evangelists, has always been the task given the church in God's mission to the world. To spread the word where it is not known or believed, to bring its comfort to those who long for a credible word in the midst of broken promises, to articulate that word in ways which truly address people in their particular needs —these are some of the tasks of evangelism.

Evangelism derives from the Greek word *euangelion*, translated into English as "gospel" or "good news." Spreading the good news is the primary responsibility of the church, for insofar as the "good news" is intimately bound up with the person and work of Jesus Christ, it is that task which distinguishes the church from all other assemblies (Augsburg Confession, Article VII., in Tappert, p. 32).

Furthermore, the church is called to continue the ministry of Jesus by proclaiming the gospel of God: "The time is fulfilled, and the kingdom of God is at hand; repent, and believe in the gospel" (Mark 1:15). Beyond that role of continuing Jesus' message, however, the church is called to proclaim Jesus Christ himself as the content of the gospel which God gives to the world.

Such proclamation within "the assembly of all believers" and outside of it—to the millions even in these United States who live day to day bereft of the gospel's comfort—is the basis for all the church does as it participates in God's mission in the world.

# CHAPTER 5

# The Church's Service to People in Need

The church in all its expressions needs further to define "the place" in which its role in God's mission is to occur. Whether that area is miles and miles of country space, the limits of a town, or a defined number of city blocks, the issue is the same: the needs of the people in the area. The area in which the church finds itself thus becomes a space where some people are nurtured by being part of the church itself. Simultaneously, such an area is a "place" where the community of Christians works beside others in a reciprocal relationship which is beneficial to all.

The service by the church works itself out in two ways. First of all, each member of that universal priesthood is equipped with the power of the gospel proclaimed in and to the community to serve others in need. Such responsibility reflects Luther's instruction to be "little Christs to the needy neighbor." Whether such "priests" are at home with family and friends or at work with business colleagues and clients, the calling to serve with the vision of the cross and of the kingdom to come is ever present. Moreover, the nature of this service, like that of Jesus at "the place," takes its form according to present needs.

Second, the institutions of the church are corporately that Body of Christ in a given area, having the responsibility of organizing themselves for effective ministry. Such organization includes ways in which the congregation or synod, for example, meets the needs of other groups of people in that locale. Whether the needs are of an emergency nature for a segment of the community devastated by flooding or fire, or the chronic hardships experienced by a socio-economic group of long-time residents, or the struggles of recent refugees, the institutions of the church need to use their corporate gifts and strengths to reach out to others in ways appropriate to their needs and consistent with the cross. According to Luther's understanding of the cross, it is indeed in such reaching out that the church finds the reality of God.

Certainly among the needs to be met by the institutions of the church are those of the vulnerable elderly. Rapidly increasing in numbers, this group of citizens is victimized in our society in a variety of ways and thus stands in need of the church's concern. Among the benevolent acts which the church as institution can render these children of God is the provision of nursing homes and other health and social services which care not only for their physical needs of shelter, food, and health care, but for their spiritual and social needs as well. Such persons need to experience that power of the gospel which defines them as human beings created in the image of God and for whom Christ died, rather than being allowed to wallow in a loss of identity because they are no longer "useful."

The same concerns for shelter, food, and health lead the institutions of the church to live out God's mission in God's world through a variety of benevolent acts, including monetary contributions and direct service. Whether those in need are the unemployed of western Pennsylvania, the Hmong community in Detroit, the Central American refugees in Los Angeles, or the oppressed in Namibia, their shelter, food, and health care are needs about which God is very much concerned and to which God sends the church. The gospel proclamation about the kingdom of

God encompasses every human need, as Jesus' own ministry demonstrates. In meeting these human needs, the church has as its primary agenda not the conversion of the beneficiaries, but solely the provision of whatever type of care is needed.

Perhaps the church needs to increase its understanding about its role in health care. Too often seen as matters of relative unimportance in the eyes of God when compared to "spiritual" needs, health and health care have not always been a priority in the church's understanding of mission.

Yet throughout the Bible, "health" and "healing" stand out as particular concerns. So common indeed is the concern about health in the biblical writings that it is completely impossible to define a specific "biblical understanding" of sickness and health. In Proverbs there are some indications that a person is rewarded with health and long life for piety and wisdom; yet the book of Job tells a story which attacks that view, leaving unanswered the question concerning the suffering of righteous people. Many of Israel's psalms were composed for use by persons afflicted with sickness, allowing them to argue with God and plead for healing. In various places it is assumed that sickness is the means by which God punishes a sinner; and yet, as we have seen, it is the afflicted and the lame, along with the outcast, who will make up the faithful remnant in the kingdom to come.

The New Testament likewise continues to reflect a variety of views regarding sickness and health. For example, Jesus healed many diseases, but Paul lingered with his thorn in the flesh. Or again, in Matthew's Gospel, the stories about Jesus' healing miracles are rooted in earthly existence itself; the healings have no figurative meaning. On the other hand, John's Gospel interprets symbolically the healing of the blind man as demonstrating "that the works of God might be made manifest in him" through this Jesus who is "the light of the world" (John 9:3, 5). On that occasion Jesus did not attribute sickness to the power of sin—

either that of the victim or of his parents (9:3). Yet the Epistle of James implies that by confessing sin, one will be healed (5:16).

All this ambivalence does not, however, leave us without some biblical understanding of sickness and healing. Clearly, sickness represents one of the disorders in God's creation caused by human sin. The first mention of pain occurs not in Genesis 1 and 2, but in the judgment pronounced on the woman in Genesis 3. Sickness and disease are, therefore, part of the universal chaos wrought by our universal sin. Not to be equated with particular manifestations of this or that person's sinfulness, sickness is one of the cosmic enemies of God which will cease in the kingdom to come.

Jesus' ministry of healing is part of his announcement about the inbreaking of the kingdom of God. "And Jesus went about all the cities and villages, teaching in their synagogues and preaching the gospel of the kingdom, and healing every disease and every infirmity" (Matthew 9:35). The healing of sickness was one of the expected transformations which would occur in the new time of God's reign. Healing is, then, the overcoming of suffering caused by universal human sin. Therefore, it is part of God's mission through the church (Matthew 10:8) to provide health care for those afflicted with disease.

Such an understanding of ministry is grounded in God's word. That word, addressed to us first at baptism, calls us into the priesthood of believers, in which we are to serve one another with sacrificial love as "little Christs" to our neighbors in various needs, including the need for health care. In addition, it is in that priesthood that some exercise their Christian vocation in such occupations as nurse, physician, and midwife—occupations which bear directly on the provision of health care. Finally, it is the priesthood of all believers which carries out a service of healing through confession and absolution, through prayer, the laying on of hands, and anointing. Through such means the whole person is treated, and only in such wholeness can healing be completed.

# CHAPTER 6

# The Church's Advocacy for Peace and Justice

Such benevolent acts as providing the needy with food, shelter, and health care are essential to God's mission. Yet the needs of people throughout the world, even on this continent, are such that the resources of the church cannot begin to serve those millions who suffer from want and oppression. Moreover, as we have seen, it is the biblical understanding that government and laws have been instituted by God for the purpose of providing some order in society, and that without laws and government to enforce those laws, chaos and anarchy would result because of human sin.

Order through laws and government is experienced when laws are just and when rulers govern justly over all people on the territory for which they have responsibility. Such laws and their enforcement, in order to be just, need not be identical with "Christian" principles or ethics, but consistent with the rights, privileges, and responsibilities of human beings of every race and creed:

> Justice may be described as distributive love. It is what God's love does when many neighbors must be served with limited resources. Justice is the form of God's creating and preserving love as that love is mediated by reason and power through persons and structures in community life. Injustice dehuman-

izes and prevents full participation in co-humanity. Justice is therefore viewed simply as that which people need to be human.

God mandates the doing of justice (Micah 6:8). The specific content of that justice, however, is not directly revealed but is discovered as life is lived amid claim and counterclaim. The discernment of justice involves every aspect of the human being. It is a task of reason, requiring the counting, measuring and classifying of factors that admit to such analysis. It is intuitive, involving the capacity for empathy. It is political, involving the struggle for power among competing groups. Above all, it is moral, involving the fundamental human capacity to know what enhances and what destroys the being and dignity of the person. That capacity, conscience, grows and is nurtured in the creative interaction of persons and groups, in the recollection of and reflection on past experience, and in the confronting of new situations.

Therefore the doing of justice is the proper stewardship of the social and material resources of creation in which our co-humanity in God's image is being realized. ("Economic Justice: Stewardship of Creation in Human Community," **Social Statements of the Lutheran Church in America** [New York: Division for Mission in North America, Lutheran Church in America, 1980], p.3.)

This understanding of justice takes seriously the in-between time in which we live—the time of new reality but also of expectation, the time of justification but also of the continuing existence of sin:

Justice takes place at the intersection of serving love and enlightened self-interest. All sinners, including Christians, are still able as the corrupted image of God to act justly out of such self-regard; and forgiven Christians are empowered to move beyond such self-regard. By the power of Christ working in them, they are freed to enlarge the conventional limits of justice ("Economic Justice," p. 4).

Defining justice is one thing, but many Christians, as well as people outside the church, have difficulty seeing the relationship of the church to the politics of justice; and so the questions continue to be asked. "Why is the church of Jesus Christ involved in such worldly concerns as unemployment or the living conditions of migrant workers?" "Is it the business of the church to concern itself with the economic impact of gambling or the abuse of women and children in their homes?" "Should the church be involved in advocating systems and laws which protect those who are unable to protect themselves?" "What is the difference between lobbying and advocacy?"

Certainly the essential task of the church is to proclaim the gospel of Jesus Christ and to administer the sacraments instituted by Christ. The gospel means, above all, that in the cross of Christ, God accepts us as children—not because of our thoughts and deeds, but in spite of them. The words of sermons and of mutual comfort among us convey this message, as do the words which interpret the signs of water in baptism and of bread and wine in the Lord's Supper. That we ourselves bring no merit of our own before God, but are called to enter the kingdom as little ones, means that we are God's children solely through God's grace and love. With nothing to offer on our own, we are—to use Luther's expression— "beggars, that is true."

Our recognition of this beggarly status enables us, in the first place, to identify with the people of God in the Old Testament. In many of the laws of ancient Israel, it is clear that Israel's former identity as slaves in Egypt and the Lord's salvation from bondage there determined why they should care for others. For the sake of the poor, the harvesters in the fields were not to be too thorough. They were commanded to leave some sheaves, olives, and grapes in the fields, for "you shall remember that you were a slave in the land of Egypt." For the same reason, Israel was responsible to God for justice due to the sojourner, the orphan, and the widow

(Deuteronomy 24:10-22).

In a similar way, those of us who know we are beggars before God can recognize our commonality with those who suffer. Just as Israel was called to identify with the needy, so we Christians can recognize our oneness with people in all conditions who have nothing to bring before God. This identification offers one motive for our role as advocates on their behalf.

Furthermore, we have seen that the purpose of God's call to Abraham—and through him to an affluent Israel—was to be a blessing for all the families of the land (Genesis 12:3). While this clause was later expanded to be a universal mission to all the "nations of the earth," and was considered by St. Paul to be "the gospel preached beforehand" (Galatians 3:8), the original purpose was to explain Israel's role in relation to the other peoples who lived on her territory. That the first example of such mediated blessing through Abraham was his advocacy for the people of Sodom is instructive for the way the Old Testament people of God conceived their role in God's mission in creation: they were called to restore the harmony and blessing, the *shalom*, of creation to others. Surely those of us who recognize the reconciliation between God and the world accomplished in Christ can see the significance of that role in God's mission. Those who cry out to God for justice and mercy are the ones for whom we speak—both to God in prayer, and to other earthly powers responsible for their well-being.

The church is called to announce in word and deed the Christ event, the event with which God broke into history to begin a new time, a reign under God which includes every creature. It is the time when those who mourn shall be comforted, when those who are confined shall be free, when the poor shall receive good news (Luke 4:18-19; 7:21-22).

Who can better serve as such agents of fortune's reversals than the church of Jesus Christ? Who has a better vision of the new day which God has in store than those who are already restored to God and to one another? Who has a more profound understanding of vulnerability than those who stand in constant need of an advocate with God?:

> My little children, I am writing this to you so that you may not sin; but if any one does sin, we have an advocate with the Father, Jesus Christ the righteous; and he is the expiation for our sins, and not for ours only but also for the sins of the whole world.
>
> (1 John 2:1-2)

This verse stands alone in the Bible in its use of the word "advocate." It describes the function which Christ serves on our behalf before God: Christ stands beside us and all people in order to intercede to God for the forgiveness of our sins.

While the English word "advocate" appears in the Bible only here, the Greek word behind it in 1 John is related to words which are translated elsewhere as "comfort" and "exhort." Indeed, the related Greek word is used in the commissioning of the prophet of the exile in the sixth century B.C.: "*Comfort, comfort* my people" with the news that their exile is over (Isaiah 40:1). It occurs again in the call of that prophet's successor, who confesses that the Lord has anointed him to "bring good news to the poor, . . . to *comfort* all who mourn" (Isaiah 61:1-2). This role of comfort (and, at times, of exhortation) is what St. Paul considers to be the task of the Christian prophet (1 Corinthians 14:1-4). Such is the task fulfilled by Paul and Barnabas (Acts 14:22), a task which belongs in the first instance to the Holy Spirit (Acts 9:31).

In all these and in many other places, the word which is translated "comfort" is directly related to the word "advocate" in 1 John 2:1. How comprehensive that activity is can be seen in the repeated use of the word at 2 Corinthians 1:3-4:

> Blessed be the God and Father of our Lord Jesus Christ, the Father of all mercies and God of all *comfort*, who *comforts* us in all affliction, so that we may be able to *comfort* those who are in any affliction, with the *comfort* with which we ourselves are *comforted* by God.

In this opening benediction to the Corinthian congregation, Paul uses the word "comfort" to speak of what God has done for us in Christ, and also of what we do for one another—for suffering and afflicted sisters and brothers. There seems to be no limit to the forms of affliction which can be met by those who have been comforted by the gospel. Perhaps this passage says, in a more specific way, what is said in that more popular verse: "We love because he first loved us."

If advocacy and comfort share the same essential meaning in these passages, then we can see that advocacy is not simply one task of the church; it is a comprehensive term for the church's ministry. Advocacy means standing beside those in need in order to speak on their behalf to others. As Christ does that for us, so we are called by God to do it for someone else.

Within the church, the family created by baptism into the death of Christ, our advocacy consists of comforting and exhorting one another *for the sake of* upbuilding and edifying. It is what Luther called "the mutual consolation" of the sisters and brothers. Such is one aspect of the advocacy role.

Simultaneously, however, the church—through its institutions and individual members—reaches out to the world for which Christ died, serving as an advocate for those "in any affliction." Those whose voices are not heard are in need of someone else to confront the powers of the world which divide people and operate solely on the basis of self-interest. In this way the church seeks to maintain the dignity of human beings created in the image of God.

As the church confronts the world for the sake of the needy, it is called to proclaim God's judgment against all who contribute to or neglect the plight of the poor. In his explanation of the Seventh Commandment in the Large Catechism, Luther makes the point strongly:

> If, when you meet a poor man who must live from hand to mouth, you act as if everyone must live by your favor, you skin and scrape him right down to the bone, and you arrogantly turn him away whom you ought to give aid, he will go away wretched and dejected, and because he can complain to no one else, he will cry to heaven. Beware of this, I repeat, as of the devil himself. Such a man's sighs and cries will be no joking matter. They will have an effect too heavy for you and all the world to bear, for they will reach God, who watches over poor, sorrowful hearts, and he will not leave them unavenged (Large Catechism, in Tappert, p. 398:247).

Luther continues:

> Our responsibility is only to instruct and reprove by means of God's word. To restrain open lawlessness is the responsibility of princes and magistrates. They should be alert and resolute enough to establish and maintain order in all areas of trade and commerce in order that the poor may not be burdened and oppressed and in order that they themselves may not be charged with other men's sins (Large Catechism, in Tappert, p. 398:249).

The church needs to determine at what point it can no longer keep silent about the injustices which result when those in authority are not "alert and resolute enough to establish and maintain order." Certainly the church must be both faithful to God's word and credible to the world as it instructs and reproves those who are responsible for justice in society. But beyond that, there are times when such a role might involve direct confrontation with civil authority, for "when commands of the civil authority cannot be obeyed without sin, we must obey God rather than men (Acts 5:29)" (*Augsburg Confession*, Article XVI., in Tappert, p. 38:7).

We have already seen that our benevolent care for the world includes feeding the hungry and clothing the destitute, providing medical care for the ill and homes for the homeless. But our advocacy also means that we identify with those "in any affliction" so that we might use whatever access to power we have in order to assure justice for our fellow human beings. Such justice goes beyond charitable giving to the point at which people are given every opportunity to maintain their human dignity, bestowed by God at the time of creation. Whether we advocate job training or child abuse laws, farm policies or decent housing, government-sponsored health care programs or protection for vulnerable sojourners, we act on behalf of people whose voices are not heard. In doing so, we carry out the work of God, who pleads the cause of the poor and despoils "of life those who despoil them" (Proverbs 22:22-23).

In this way, advocacy is distinguished from lobbying. While both aim to influence members of a legislative body in matters of legislation or policy, the difference appears in whom they represent. While a lobbyist is a representative of a particular interest group, an advocate is one who speaks not for oneself or for an isolated group, but for all people, so that the rights of all members of society may be maintained. Such advocacy in matters political must not attempt to influence decisions along Christian or partisan lines, but solely in terms of human justice. Using the church's energy and finances to bring to our own day a vision of the kingdom to come is not peripheral, but essential to God's mission in the world.

To play such a role in the world on behalf of God's mission requires not only the motive of the gospel, but also diligent study of the issues. It is here, in this direct encounter with the power structures of the world, that the church needs to call upon its resources of reason and research. The church will have no credibility among those who govern unless it speaks with some of the intellectual capacity which God bestowed upon humanity at the time of creation. It is with this reason and wisdom that we are to be responsible stewards of God's creation, and it is with people of like minds that the church needs to cooperate in order to be comprehensive in terms of expertise and powerful in terms of persuasion.

If the church is to be an effective advocate for the vulnerable of the earth, it must function in the realm of the powerful. Therein lies a tension for the church. The approach to our ministry, we have seen, is one of weakness and vulnerability; it is the sacrificing way of the cross. Yet in order to be effective in advocating justice, the church must exercise its corporate power. The two approaches are not in contradiction. The church has a responsibility to identify with the poor and oppressed, the suffering and the helpless, the sick and the lonely. It is out of that identification that the church uses its corporate power to attain access to the powerful. Indeed, it is only for the sake of others that the church has any right to exert power, for the church is called by God to continue the work of the crucified Christ.

Advocacy within and outside the church is always a matter of comfort and exhortation. It is, as the word expresses, the role of speaking to someone on another's behalf. Surely the needy of the world must have some advocate willing to take risks on their behalf. No one should know that better than we sinners for whom Christ died, and for whom Christ continues to be an advocate.

# CHAPTER 7

# The Church's Teaching Role

While a distinction is often made between *kerygma* and *didache*, between Sunday morning sermons and instruction, between preaching and teaching, it is difficult to maintain that distinction in actual practice. A sermon has as its primary purpose to proclaim the word of God in such a way that the audience will experience the judging and saving presence of God, that is, law and gospel; but such a sermon will likely teach the audience something about the human condition and its manifestations in contemporary life, and about the nature of the God as revealed through the witness of Scripture. Likewise, a teaching session about the Bible, the nature of the church, or a social issue can be the vehicle by which one experiences the law-gospel encounter with God, even though the primary objective of the teacher might be the distribution of information.

Seen in this light, the role of teaching within the church and its function within God's mission is all-encompassing. The education of the constituency in every expression of the church and in all its endeavors goes hand in hand with the proclamation of the gospel: that outreach of the church through word and sacrament.

The content of such education within the church is likewise virtually limitless. In order for the church to be God's people in the world, any or all of the issues discussed in this paper might comprise the content of curricula which are developed for use in congregations, in coalitions, in synods, or even throughout the church nationwide. Whether specifically related to Bible study, to the nature of the church, to the meaning of justification, or, more broadly, to creation and justice issues such as racism, sexism, economics, ecology, politics, peace and war, or various global problems, all such content can contribute to that constituency's understanding of God's mission through the church. Whether or not such a contribution is made depends in large part on the ability of the teacher or of the course to relate God's redemption and God's creation as inseparable issues for the church. In other words, the constituency needs to understand the relationship between the gospel proclamation and the worldly context in which and to which the gospel is proclaimed in word and deed. Only in this way can the church be effective in fulfilling its mandate for mission.

One of the many issues requiring a close relationship between gospel proclamation and teaching responsibility is that of inclusiveness and diversity in the church and the consequent role of the church in combating racism in society. The church's role in God's mission in terms of its "outreach through word and sacrament" must, without reservation or condition, include people of every color and race. Indeed, the church realizes itself as the eschatological miracle of God's reign when it announces and experiences the inclusiveness of God's justification and the blessed diversity of God's creation. In order to avoid equating that word of God with the words and expressions of a particular culture, the church must be that inclusive and diverse community in which worship and proclamation assume different languages and forms, so long as those differences do not obscure the unity of the family's understanding of word and sacrament. It is that criterion, and that alone, which defines the church.

Because of the persistence of sin in all, including those in the church, the issue of race is vital for the church's teaching ministry. As teacher, the church needs to combat by education the biases and prejudices which can prevent even its own membership from including people of different color and language. That education includes insights from the Bible, like those issues discussed earlier in this paper, but it needs also to include a direct response to the racial stereotypes and attitudes which keep people apart. The church needs to instruct its own constituency that the nature of the gospel and of the kingdom of God does not coincide with attitudes based on prejudice and with discrimination based upon ignorance. These are teaching concerns which the church cannot simply leave to others because Christians, people whose minds have been renewed, have some deep insights into the nature of God's creation and of all people created in the image of God.

It is that insight into God's creation and the role of the people of God in the world that leads the church to move out beyond preaching and teaching about inclusiveness in order to address the world concerning racial justice. Through its gathering of data and through its cooperation with other groups and institutions, the church seeks to understand the social implications and effects of racism on people of color and language. In this way, the church joins other groups with like concerns and interests in the pursuit of justice. Whether dealing with the effects of racial discrimination in the realms of education, employment and layoff policies, health care and food stamps, or housing and zoning laws, the church's concern for benevolence and justice needs to be clear and consistent. When properly educated about the issues, Christians individually and collectively can be effective advocates for those who are oppressed, not in order to convert people to church membership, but in order to provide on behalf of the Creator the justice due to people on the basis of their rights as human beings made in God's image.

Another issue which requires a combination of the church's

preaching and teaching is that of sexuality. On the basis of God's creation, and out of its understanding of the power of God's redemption, the church recognizes its responsibility in preaching and teaching the word of God in relation to sexual equality. To do otherwise is to allow human sin, rather than God's action, to determine the role given to the church. In terms of its preaching, the church proclaims to those who continue to subjugate and dominate women not only the gospel of forgiveness, but also the gospel of the kingdom whereby sexual equality is restored "in Christ." The two-edged nature of the word simultaneously convicts all who attempt to continue, explicitly and implicitly, the hierarchy of the sexes which is overcome by God's grace bestowed in baptism. "There is neither male nor female; for you are all one in Christ Jesus."

In preaching that message and in the teaching of the whole biblical story (rather than citing isolated proof texts) about sexuality, the church needs to be wary of the danger of falling back into sexism. In the context of worship or in any other activity within the church, the use of language which excludes women must be avoided; the use of illustrations in preaching and teaching needs to be balanced. Even the way the church speaks of God ought to reflect the diversity of images in the Bible itself; that is, not only the title "father," but the imagery so common in the Old Testament which portrays God in motherly terms (e.g., Deuteronomy 32:18; Isaiah 49:15; Isaiah 66:13), used also by Jesus in the telling of parables (Matthew 23:37; cf. also Luke 15:8-10).

Beyond its preaching and teaching in regard to sexual equality, the church as an institution needs to reflect within itself the eschatological vision of oneness in Christ Jesus. The leadership of the church, both clergy and laity, should reflect the makeup of its membership at all levels of the institution, from church councils on the congregational level to national committees and boards, and even to the offices of bishop.

From that vantage point the church can be a credible advocate for equality in terms of male and female roles in society. In regard to such issues as employment and salary, job training and opportunity, income tax and social security laws, insurance coverage and financial credit practices, the church needs to be involved, not in order to assert "Christian" principles on the basis of redemption, but to promote justice on the basis of creation. Furthermore, the church needs to oppose through its advocacy all manifestations of sexism in areas such as advertising where women are used as objects of manipulation or humor which is often demeaning to the female sex. The church needs to exert, without reservation, its dual responsibilities of service and justice in addressing the violent abuse of women in the home and in society. Working alongside other groups, the church can be an effective agent in changing attitudes and practices toward women in the world.

At the same time, the church needs to set in balance a concern for men at various levels. In terms of preaching the word of God and teaching the meaning of mission under the cross, the church faces a number of issues, some of which are the result of traditional sexual roles. Proclaiming forgiveness and reconciliation to a man who regards these messages as a threat to his masculinity is a challenge to the preacher. Furthermore, the description of the church's mission as informed by a theology of the cross presents a dilemma, for such a theology of limitation, weakness, and vulnerability represents characteristics traditionally assigned to women. Clearly, the church needs to consider such challenges if it is to be inclusive of men while faithful to its understanding of the gospel.

In addition, the growing number of broken marriages in our day inflicts pain on men and women alike. It is part of the church's role in God's mission to seek just laws and practices and to educate in terms of human dynamics.

Whether the issues be those of just and equitable financial

support or custody and visitation of children, both men and women have been and still are treated harshly in many courts of law. The church's outreach of the word in terms of comfort, the church's need to educate in regard to responsible parenting and cooperative efforts of divorced spouses, the church's pursuit of justice through advocacy -- all these converge when the church is willing to face the realities of familial brokenness.

The issues of race and sexuality here provide examples of how the preaching and teaching functions of the church interrelate and, further, how those functions lead to the involvement of the church in service and in the pursuit of justice through advocacy.

## The Church and Higher Education

Even though the Christian is called upon by Paul to "be transformed by the renewal of your mind," there is no attempt in the Bible to urge the forsaking of worldly wisdom. On the contrary, in different ways the biblical writers affirm worldly wisdom even while they simultaneously deny the possibility of its use to know God or to discern God's mind.

Our insights gleaned from the Bible and the Lutheran Confessions are consistent in their understanding that human wisdom plays no role in justification, but contributes to the responsible stewardship of daily life in the realm of creation. Since, as we have indicated in several ways throughout this document, the Christian and the church cannot ignore the world or escape the tasks given by the Creator. Neither can the church escape the necessity for worldly wisdom and for promoting the increase of wisdom through education as a task assigned by God to all creatures made in God's image:

> This means that education in general, and the church-related college in particular, have an integrity and purpose grounded in the Creed's first Article, concerning Creation. The capacity to learn -- to search into the secrets of nature and perceive our

misery and grandeur, to search into the riddle of history and be stalkers of meaning -- is possible because of God's goodness. The fact that sinners are not justified by knowledge or cultural refinement should not obscure the further fact that education is the gift of a loving Creator. Through it he would enhance and enrich people's lives. Through it he would inform, motivate and equip them to make human society what he intends it to be. Sound scholarship, careful research, and effective teaching do him honor and serve his cause.

This perception of education, grounded in the theology of the Lutheran church, establishes the freedom and significance of educational institutions. It affirms the college as a college, devoted to its primary task, blending together the differing talents and convictions of many persons.

This understanding also makes clear that it is both unbiblical and misleading to speak of "Christian" higher education or a "Christian" college. ("The Basis for Partnership between Church and College," **A Statement of the Lutheran Church in America** [New York: Division for Mission in North America, Lutheran Church in America, 1980], pp. 4-5.)

To carry the thought one step further, there is no such thing as "Christian" biology, mathematics, or chemistry. The disciplines of education are matters in which Christians join with others to pursue those things which are of the world, of creation, and therefore of God's concern. Yet, while the Christian cannot allow one's faith to stand in the way of scientific research or dynamic teaching, that same faith does provide a perspective out of which one studies, teaches, and learns. In a world uncertain of its values or dedicated to "objective" dissemination of information, the Christian and the church-related college work to provide "a corporate forum in which to speak the truth in love and to bear a corporate witness to the sacredness of the secular world" ("The Basis for Partnership between Church and College," p. 7).

Furthermore, while not attempting to infuse worldly disciplines with "Christian" principles, the church-related college does provide the church with opportunities for its mission. Certainly the office of the chaplain and the opportunity for worship in such a setting make possible that first concern of the church, namely, to reach out to people through word and sacrament. Indeed, the chaplain's office itself adds another dimension to the counseling of students in personal matters: a perspective of the gospel from which to live out life in its conflicts. In addition, because academic or intellectual expertise is necessary to understand the complexities of various social issues, the church-related college and its resources contribute to the mission of the church in its pursuit of justice through advocacy. That same expertise in worldly matters is no less important for the church if it is to preach the word adequately and relevantly.

On the level of worldly wisdom, the college offers to the church an immediate contact with the diversity of people and of thought, diversity which can challenge the church's theological traditions and result in constructive dialogue, enabling the church better to understand the wholeness of God's world. Such benefits to the church are by no means automatic, and so the church must be aggressive in its attempt to receive the advantages which college relationships have to offer.

> The college serves God's world well when it consciously and deliberately prepares people to be responsible citizens. It serves both the church and God's world well when it consciously and deliberately prepares Christians to live their baptism in the world ("The Basis for Partnership between Church and College," p. 9).

# SUMMARY

The church of Jesus Christ, called into being by the Holy Spirit, is defined in the ancient ecumenical creeds as "the communion of saints" and as "one[,] holy, catholic and apostolic." The Lutheran confessional statements continue these understandings while simultaneously offering a definition of the church as that "assembly of believers among whom the Gospel is preached in its purity and the holy sacraments are administered according to the Gospel" (Augsburg Confession, Article VII., in Tappert, p. 32).

While it is assumed in these statements, the role of the church in God's mission is not explicitly defined. However, the biblical evidence offers us ample testimony to pursue the nature of this role in relation to God's command. One of the themes which is consistent throughout Holy Scripture is that of the kingdom or reign of God. Experienced by ancient Israel both in terms of God's creation and in relation to redemption, the kingdom of God eventually took on exclusively future expectations. Contrary to Israel's present experience, that "day of the Lord" would be a time for the reversal of fortunes, especially for the poor and the oppressed.

The New Testament bears witness to the inbreaking of this kingdom in the life, death, and resurrection of Jesus Christ. The expected transformations of "that day" were already occurring, and the evidence for this new time was the birth of the church. Thus the church represents to the world that new reality; as such the church is called to proclaim the gospel of Jesus Christ and the kingdom of God and, at the same time, to be the sign of what the kingdom was expected to be.

Simultaneously, because of the persistence of sin in humankind, even in those called to be the church, it was obvious that the reign of God was not yet complete. And so, the same New Testament witness looked forward to the final consummation of God's reign in the future. Thus the church found itself—and still does find itself—as the assembly which is "in the world," but not "of the world," belonging as it does to the heavenly commonwealth.

It is in this tension of the two times that God's mission through the church is carried out. Manifesting the new reality in the world, the church approaches the world, not with hostility, but with hospitality. Its strategy for reaching out to the world can be no different from that of Jesus Christ, particularly as his ministry came to culmination on the cross at Golgotha. It is, therefore, on the basis of the theology of the cross, a theology of service and sacrifice, weakness and vulnerability, and identification with the suffering that the church reaches out to the world.

In that broken world God's mission consists of the church's outreach through word and sacrament, service to people in need, peace and justice through advocacy, and a teaching role in relation to its own. These aspects of mission cannot be separated, for they overlap and complement one another in every activity. The world's needs and the opportunities for the church's ministry are such that all aspects of God's mission work interdependently.

Such an approach to mission takes God's creation seriously as the arena in which redeemed Christians live out their baptismal vocation. The world is not, as in radical apocalyptic thinking, the evil realm which must be avoided. While the world represents the former time, it is not automatically the object of the church's attack. The world—broken and sinful—is the realm over which God rules through laws, institutions, governing authorities, and human reason. The church, therefore, with a renewed mind, approaches the often hostile world with a sense of justice for all people which goes beyond the normal limits of human justice.

This understanding of the world and God's mission prevents us from placing the entire discussion of mission in the realm of redemption. On the one hand, this means that it is not our primary task to make the world "Christian," for the responsibility of changing the world into the kingdom of God belongs to God alone, and is reserved for that future which is in God's hands. On the other hand, we cannot identify every victory for social justice, every liberation from oppression, every manifestation of human cooperation, as redemptive. Redemption is the act of God in forgiving sin and thereby restoring that relationship between God and humans which was broken on "the afternoon of the first day." The social and political freedoms which occur in the world are matters which relate to the other broken relationships—that of humans to one another in society, that of humans to the world, and even that of God to the earth. These are matters of creation and of justice, rather than of redemption.

To distinguish these two concerns—that of redemption and that of creation and justice—in no way allows the Christian or the church to separate them in terms of God's mission. On the contrary, those who are equipped with renewed minds are sent into the world. It is they who realize that the church itself is not the end of God's will and work, but the means by which God reaches out to the world until the time when God will make all things new. Until that time the church participates in God's mission under the cross of Jesus Christ and with hope in the resurrection promised to those who believe.